GREAT EXPECTATIONS

AN ESSAY WRITING GUIDE FOR GCSE

BY ASHLEIGH WEIR

SERIES EDITOR: R. P. DAVIS

First published in 2020 by Accolade Tuition Ltd
71-75 Shelton Street
Covent Garden
London WC2H 9JQ
www.accoladetuition.com
info@accoladetuition.com

ISBN 978-1-913988-00-5

FIRST EDITION
1 3 5 7 9 10 8 6 4 2

CONTENTS

EDITOR'S FOREWORD

In your GCSE English Literature exam, you will be presented with an extract from Charles Dickens' *Great Expectations* and a question that asks you to offer both a close analysis of the extract plus a commentary of the novel as a whole. Of course, there are many methods one *might* use to tackle this style of question. However, there is one particular technique which, due to its sophistication, most readily allows students to unlock the highest marks: namely, **the thematic method**.

To be clear, this study guide is *not* intended to walk you through the novel scene-by-scene: there are many great guides out there that do just that. No, this guide, by sifting through a series of mock exam questions, will demonstrate *how* to organise a response thematically and thus write a stellar essay: a skill we believe no other study guide adequately covers!

I have encountered students who have structured their essays all sorts of ways: some by writing about the extract line by line, others by identifying various language techniques and giving each its own paragraph. The method I'm advocating, on the other hand, involves picking out three to four themes that will allow you to holistically answer the question: these three to four themes will become the three to four content paragraphs of your essay, cushioned between a brief introduction and conclusion. Ideally, these themes will follow from one to the next to create a flowing argument. Within each of these thematic paragraphs, you can then ensure you are jumping through the mark scheme's hoops.

So to break things down further, each thematic paragraph will include various point-scoring components. In each paragraph, you will quote from the extract, offer analyses of these quotes, then discuss how the specific language techniques you have identified illustrate the theme you're discussing. In each paragraph, you will also discuss how other parts of the novel further illustrate the theme (or even complicate it). And in each, you will comment on the era in which the novel was written and how that helps to understand the chosen theme.

Don't worry if this all feels daunting. Throughout this book, the very talented Ashleigh (the author!) will be illustrating in great detail – by means of examples – how to build an essay of this kind.

Charles Dickens.

The Dickensian equivalent of a selfie.

The beauty of the thematic approach is that, once you have your themes, you suddenly have a direction and a trajectory, and this makes essay writing a whole lot easier. However, it must also be noted that extracting themes in the first place is something students often find tricky. I have come across many candidates who understand the extract and the novel inside out; but when they are presented with a question under exam conditions, and the pressure kicks in, they find it tough to break their response down into themes. The fact of the matter is: the process is a *creative* one and the best themes require a bit of imagination.

In this guide, Ashleigh shall take seven different exam-style questions, coupled with extracts from the novel, and put together a plan for each – a plan that illustrates in detail how we will be satisfying the mark scheme's criteria. Please do keep in mind that, when operating under timed conditions, your plans will necessarily be less detailed than those that appear in this volume.

Now, you might be asking whether three or four themes is best. The truth is, you should do whatever you feel most comfortable with: the examiner is looking for an original, creative answer, and not sitting there counting the themes. So if you think you are quick enough to cover four, then great. However, if you would rather do three to make sure you do each theme justice, that's also fine. I sometimes suggest that my student pick four themes, but make the fourth one smaller – sort of like an afterthought, or an observation that turns things on their head. That way, if they feel they won't have time to explore this fourth theme in its own right, they can always give it a quick mention in the conclusion instead.

A London mural of Charles Dickens, surrounded by his fictional characters.

Before I hand you over to Ashleigh, I believe it to be worthwhile to run through the four Assessment Objectives the exam board want you to cover in your response – if only to demonstrate how effective the thematic response can be. I would argue that the first Assessment Objective (AO1) – the one that wants candidates to 'read, understand and respond to texts' and which is worth 12 of the total 34 marks up for grabs – will be wholly satisfied by selecting strong themes, then fleshing them out with quotes. Indeed, when it comes to identifying the top-scoring candidates for AO1, the mark scheme explicitly tells examiners to look for a 'critical, exploratory, conceptualised response' that makes 'judicious use of precise references' – the word 'concept' is a synonym of theme, and 'judicious references' simply refers to quotes that appropriately support the theme you've chosen.

The second Assessment Objective (AO2) – which is also responsible for 12 marks – asks students to 'analyse the language, form and structure used by a writer to create meanings and effects, using relevant subject terminology where appropriate.' As noted, you will already be quoting from the novel as you back up your themes, and it is a natural progression to then analyse the language techniques used. In fact, this is far more effective than simply observing language techniques (personification here, alliteration there), because by discussing how the language techniques relate to and shape the theme, you will also be demonstrating how the writer 'create[s] meanings and effects.'

Now, in my experience, language analysis is the most important element of AO2 – perhaps 8 of the 12 marks will go towards language analysis. You will also notice, however, that AO2 asks students to comment on 'form and structure.' Again, the thematic approach has your back – because though simply jamming in a point on form or structure will feel jarring, when you bring these points up while discussing a theme, as a means to further a thematic argument, you will again organically be discussing the way it 'create[s] meanings and effects.'

AO3 requires you to 'show understanding of the relationships between texts and the contexts in which they were written' and is responsible for a more modest 6 marks in total. These are easy enough to weave into a thematic argument; indeed, the theme gives the student a chance to bring up context in a relevant and fitting way. After all, you don't want it to look like you've just shoehorned a contextual factoid into the mix.

Finally, you have AO4 – known also as "spelling and grammar." There are four marks up for grabs here. Truth be told, this guide is not geared towards AO4. My advice? Make sure you are reading plenty of books and articles, because the more you read, the better your spelling and grammar will be. Also, before the exam, perhaps make a list of words you struggle to spell but often find yourself using in essays, and commit them to memory.

The front facade of Dickens's first London home, situated in Fitzrovia.

My (and Ashleigh's) hope is that this book, by demonstrating how to tease out themes from an extract, will help you feel more confident in doing so yourself. I believe it is also worth mentioning that the themes Ashleigh has picked out are by no means definitive. Asked the very same question, someone else may pick out different themes, and write an answer that is just as good (if not better!). Obviously the exam is not likely to be fun – my memory of them is pretty much the exact opposite. But still, this is one of the very few chances that you will get at GCSE level to actually be creative. And to my mind at least, that was always more enjoyable – if *enjoyable* is the right word

– than simply demonstrating that I had memorised loads of facts.

R. P. Davis, Series Editor

READ THE FOLLOWING EXTRACT FROM
CHAPTER 5 OF GREAT EXPECTATIONS
AND THEN ANSWER THE QUESTION THAT
FOLLOWS.

A t this point in the novel, Joe and Pip have just
accompanied the soldiers as they recaptured
the escaped convicts.

My convict never looked at me, except that once. While we
stood in the hut, he stood before the fire looking thoughtfully at
it, or putting up his feet by turns upon the hob, and looking
thoughtfully at them as if he pitied them for their recent adven-
tures. Suddenly, he turned to the sergeant, and remarked,—

"I wish to say something respecting this escape. It may prevent
some persons laying under suspicion alonger me."

"You can say what you like," returned the sergeant, standing
coolly looking at him with his arms folded, "but you have no
call to say it here. You'll have opportunity enough to say about
it, and hear about it, before it's done with, you know."

"I know, but this is another pint, a separate matter. A man can't starve; at least *I* can't. I took some wittles, up at the willage over yonder,—where the church stands a'most out on the marshes."

"You mean stole," said the sergeant.

"And I'll tell you where from. From the blacksmith's."

"Halloa!" said the sergeant, staring at Joe.

"Halloa, Pip!" said Joe, staring at me.

"It was some broken wittles—that's what it was—and a dram of liquor, and a pie."

"Have you happened to miss such an article as a pie, black-smith?" asked the sergeant, confidentially.

"My wife did, at the very moment when you came in. Don't you know, Pip?"

"So," said my convict, turning his eyes on Joe in a moody manner, and without the least glance at me,—"so you're the blacksmith, are you? Than I'm sorry to say, I've eat your pie."

"God knows you're welcome to it,—so far as it was ever mine," returned Joe, with a saving remembrance of Mrs. Joe. "We don't know what you have done, but we wouldn't have you starved to death for it, poor miserable fellow-creatur.—Would us, Pip?"

Starting with this moment in the play, ~~play,~~ *novel* **explore how Dickens presents the relationship between generosity and class.**

Write about:

- **how Dickens presents the relationship**

between generosity and class at this moment in the novel.

• **how Dickens presents the relationship between generosity and class in the novel as a whole.**

Introduction

Here you are being asked to focus on two specific concepts in relation to one another. While both are massively important in the novel, it is important that you treat both equally in the time you have, so make sure you choose examples where you have interesting things to say about both class and generosity. Notice also how I invoke two other of Dickens' novels in the introduction below, thereby scoring AO3 (contextual) marks off the bat.

"Dickens was incredibly invested in the importance of charity. Many of his novels (*A Christmas Carol, Oliver Twist*) centre themselves around the value of generosity and how it can affect the lives of the poor and needy for the better. In *Great Expectations*, Dickens explores the implications of generosity between classes and how the act of both giving and receiving differs according to social circumstance."

Theme/Paragraph One: Generosity is presented as being worth more when it comes from those who have nothing.

- Generosity can be seen as requiring a level of self sacrifice, of giving something up in order to better the position of someone else. When a person who has little to give is generous, their generosity could be considered far more significant than someone of greater means. The Gargery family are among the lower class characters in the novel; they are uneducated, live in 'a wooden house' and dine on 'bread and butter'. Dickens writes their dialogue pseudo-phonetically in order to signpost their regional dialect and lack of elocution.[1] In the above extract, Joe's kindness towards Magwitch's confession of theft can be seen as generous, especially since, compared with some of the other characters in the novel, his position could itself be considered as needy. Dickens here draws similarities to the biblical story of the Widow's Offering in Luke 21:1-4.[2] [*AO1 for advancing the argument with a judiciously selected quote; AO2 for the close analysis of the language; AO3 for placing the text in literary-historical context*].

- In spite of the nature of Magwitch's unknown crime, Joe remarks that he 'wouldn't have [him] starved to death for it' and describes the convict as a 'poor miserable fellow-creatur'. Although he is by no means equal in wealth or social standing, Joe recognises his equality in humanity with the word 'fellow'. Magwitch has been stripped of his human refinement while Joe maintains his. Joe's generosity can therefore be seen as a recognition of this fundamental commonality. [*AO1 for advancing the argument with a judiciously selected quote*]

Theme/Paragraph Two: It is expected that

generosity must flow from a higher class to a lower class, from those that have to those who have not. Throughout the novel, Dickens redirects this flow.

- In the extract above, Magwitch's confession can be seen as an act of generosity in return for Pip's having brought him the 'broken wittles' and 'dram of liquor'. In this instance, Dickens explores the insinuation that the flow of generosity from those that have to those who have not does not necessarily automatically involve class. Here, for example, Pip is Magwitch's social superior, but Magwitch is more circumstantially powerful, as he has the ability to out Pip as a thief. His choice not only to retain Pip's secret but to furthermore protect him by taking responsibility for the stolen food is an act of generosity that is not linked to material wealth. [*AO1 for advancing the argument with a judiciously selected quote*].

- Elsewhere in the novel: The interweaved themes of generosity and class between Magwitch and Pip come into play again later in the novel in a more material way when Magwitch reveals himself as Pip's benefactor. Pip reacts with 'repugnance' in response. It is undoubtedly Pip's advancement in class that instinctively rejects Magwitch's generosity, as having unknowingly accepted patronage from a criminal undermines his social expectations. Here the relationship between class and generosity is fraught, as rather than a person of low status accepting generosity from a person of higher status (as was acceptable and socially encouraged), Pip as a gentleman has been accepting generosity from a vagrant-class criminal. When Pip assumes Miss

Havisham to be his patron, the flow of generosity seems far more socially acceptable; here, however, the flow has been redirected. [*AO1 for advancing the argument with a judiciously selected quote*]

Theme/Paragraph Three: Generosity is dubiously transactional. Though one should not expect recompense or reciprocal generosity in return, gratitude is the expected response to generosity and failure to behave gratefully is shunned by various characters throughout the novel.

- Elsewhere in the novel: Ingratitude is presented as a flaw in the novel, to which no class is immune. Pip later expresses regret for his aforementioned repulsion, and rather than seeing a criminal in Magwitch, he remarks 'I only saw a man who had meant to be my benefactor, and who had felt affectionately, gratefully, and generously, towards me with great constancy through a series of years.' That Magwitch is described as both grateful and generous connotes a further biblical tone in the notion that generosity breeds generosity, with gratitude functioning as the intermediate. [*AO1 for advancing the argument with a judiciously selected quote*]
- However, the expectation of gratitude could itself be seen to undermine a benefactor's generosity, as generosity that obligates a certain behaviour from its receiver is transactional, not simply charitable. When Estella is described as an 'ingrate' by her benefactor Miss Havisham after she behaves indifferently

towards her, she retorts that 'I have said that I owe everything to you. All I possess is freely yours. All that you have given me, is at your command to have again.', the implication being that she did not ask for Miss Havisham's patronage, and therefore is under no obligation to serve her in any particular way, despite Miss Havisham's desires.

- Conversely, when Magwitch reveals himself, he assures Pip, 'Do I tell it, fur you to feel a obligation? Not a bit', merely to know that he had made him 'a gentleman'. Indeed, Magwitch's unconditional generosity is arguably prefigured in this extract, since the way he avoids 'the least glance at' Pip while dissembling on his behalf could symbolise his lack of expectation for anything in return for his kindness; indeed, that his disinclination to look at Pip is mentioned at the very start of the passage grants it additional structural emphasis, too [3] Generosity with strings attached is arguably not generosity at all, but rather investment, and it seems throughout the novel that Dickens presents the characters of higher classes as being far less willing to give without hope of return. [AO1 for advancing the argument with a judiciously selected quote; AO2 for the close analysis of the language and for discussing how structure shapes meaning]

Conclusion

Although I'm happy with the themes we've dealt with in this essay, I have a sense that I may be lacking slightly on the AO3 (historical) side of things. As a result, I've decided to invoke another nineteenth century text as a means to ensure those marks do not fall through the cracks!

"At the outset of Charlotte Bronte's *Jane Eyre,* the eponymous and lowly protagonist is on the receiving end of a deeply dubious act of charity: her wealthy aunt takes her in, but only on the condition of fawning obsequiousness and gratitude.[4] *Great Expectations,* by drawing attention to the hollowness of generosity that seeks gratitude in return, explores a similar fault-line in the relationship between class and generosity. However, not only does Dickens draw attention to how charity can be perverted, he also, through the character of Magwitch, challenges assumptions of the flow of generosity between social classes."

A poster for David Lean's 1946 film adaptation of *Great Expectations*.

ESSAY PLAN TWO

READ THE FOLLOWING EXTRACT FROM
CHAPTER 14 OF GREAT EXPECTATIONS
AND THEN ANSWER THE QUESTION THAT
FOLLOWS.

At this point in the novel, Pip has just returned home having visited the home of Miss Havisham for the last time and has been bound as Joe's apprentice.

It is a most miserable thing to feel ashamed of home. There may be black ingratitude in the thing, and the punishment may be retributive and well deserved; but that it is a miserable thing, I can testify.

Home had never been a very pleasant place to me, because of my sister's temper. But, Joe had sanctified it, and I had believed in it. I had believed in the best parlour as a most elegant saloon; I had believed in the front door, as a mysterious portal of the Temple of State whose solemn opening was attended with a sacrifice of roast fowls; I had believed in the kitchen as a chaste though not magnificent apartment; I had believed in the forge as the glowing road to manhood and independence. Within a single year all this was changed. Now it was all coarse and common, and I would not have had Miss Havisham and Estella see it on any account.

How much of my ungracious condition of mind may have been my own fault, how much Miss Havisham's, how much my sister's, is now of no moment to me or to any one. The change was made in me; the thing was done. Well or ill done, excusably or inexcusably, it was done.

Once, it had seemed to me that when I should at last roll up my shirt-sleeves and go into the forge, Joe's 'prentice, I should be distinguished and happy. Now the reality was in my hold, I only felt that I was dusty with the dust of small-coal, and that I had a weight upon my daily remembrance to which the anvil was a feather. There have been occasions in my later life (I suppose as in most lives) when I have felt for a time as if a thick curtain had fallen on all its interest and romance, to shut me out from anything save dull endurance any more. Never has that curtain dropped so heavy and blank, as when my way in life lay stretched out straight before me through the newly entered road of apprenticeship to Joe.

Starting with this moment in the novel, explore how far Dickens presents Pip as ashamed of his social standing. Write about:

• how Dickens presents Pip's shame at this moment in the novel.

• how Dickens presents Pip's shame in the novel as a whole.

Introduction

This question might initially seem simple; you don't need to mine the text too much to find evidence of Pip's shame about home. However, as a result of this, it is important that you take especial care to include solid AO2 analysis.

> "Pip is presented as being ashamed of a number of things throughout the novel. He is ashamed of his childhood secret, of his persistent connection to Magwitch, and indeed of his upbringing and low social standing. *Great Expectations* is a bildungsroman, or coming-of-age story, and much of Pip's personal journey involves coming to terms with his shame and the implications of his social advancement and how it affects his appreciation of himself and those he encounters."[1]

Theme/Paragraph One: Shame comes in response to gaining insight into a more privileged class of life which exposes his own as 'coarse and common'.

- Pip is not presented as having always felt ashamed of his social standing. Although he concedes that 'Home had never been a very pleasant place' to him, Dickens portrays him reminiscing about his former fondness of the place. Dickens' descriptions of Pip's past appreciation of home are rich and fantastical and slightly hyperbolic; the door is a 'mysterious portal' at

which 'roast fowls' were sacrificed with great
solemnity and the parlour he imagines as a 'most
elegant saloon'.[2] It is his exposure to the luxury of
Miss Havisham's home that renders him subsequently
unable to see these articles so glamorously. While he
was able to traverse between the worlds of the
Gargery household and Miss Havisham's manse, this
is not so much of a problem. However, now that he is
literally 'bound' to Joe and the forge, with no hope of
returning to Miss Havisham or enjoying that lifestyle
again, he has been left with the ability to appreciate
his social standing in contrast to a better one of which
he now can never be a part. [*AO1 for advancing the
argument with a judiciously selected quote; AO2 for
the close analysis of the language*].

- Dickens' use of tense is integral to his presentation of
Pip's shame about his social standing. In the extract
above, he makes extensive use of the anaphora 'I had
believed'; 'I had believed in the best parlour as a most
elegant saloon; I had believed in the front door as a
mysterious portal' etc.[3] The pluperfect tense holds
insinuations of a further action, still in the past, which
contrasts, furthers or contradicts the previous action.[4]
The repetition of this pluperfect anaphora is
relentless; it is four richly descriptive clauses within
one long sentence. The contrasting action suggested
by the tense, however— 'Within a single year all this
was changed'— is somewhat bathetic.[5] It is a stark and
short sentence, perhaps depicting how years and years
of belief were waylaid so swiftly and simply. Dickens
further compounds this with his description of it as a
drop of a curtain, 'heavy and blank'; a single finalising
action that cannot be undone. [*AO1 for advancing the

argument with a judiciously selected quote; AO2 for
the close analysis of the language and for discussing
how form shapes meaning].

Theme/Paragraph Two: There is a distinction
between the narrator's viewpoint and that of his
younger self. By the end of the novel, Pip is
humbler and has come to better terms with his
social background.

- Pip continues to feel shame around the social standing
  of his childhood as the novel progresses. He confides
  in Biddy that he hopes to become a gentleman, and in
  Chapter 19 confesses that he finds Joe's manners
  coarse and embarrassing. However, much later in the
  novel, he is forced to reconsider his attitude towards
  his upbringing and its social standing and in some
  ways can be seen to be ashamed of his shame. This
  can be seen in the tone of narration in the extract
  above when this shame is described as an 'ungracious
  condition'. [*AO1 for advancing the argument with a*
  judiciously selected quote; AO2 for discussing how
  structure shapes meaning].
- Because *Great Expectations* is written with a first
  person retrospective narration, there is a distinction
  between Pip's omniscience as an older narrator and
  the perspective of the narrated Pip as a child.[6] In the
  extract above, Pip the narrator speaks of his child-
  self's shame with a mixture of pity and disapproval:
  'There may be black ingratitude in the thing, and the
  punishment may be retributive and well deserved; but
  that it is a miserable thing, I can testify.' The personal

identification with the hardship of his past re-emerges at the end of the extract when he likens his experience of a 'thick curtain' shutting out 'interest and romance' at times in his 'later life' to his experience of this moment as a child, and, in fact, concedes that it was worse in this instance: 'Never has that curtain dropped so heavy and blank, as when my way in life lay stretched out straight before me through the newly entered road of apprenticeship to Joe.' [*AO1 for advancing the argument with a judiciously selected quote; AO2 for the close analysis of the language*].

Theme/Paragraph Three: Pip's shame is tightly allied with expectations of masculinity.

- In the Victorian era, it was expected that men and women would adhere to very specific, separate roles in society, and those roles – though no less separate – differed between classes. Generally, women enjoyed lower status and fewer rights than the men within their class who were expected to be the breadwinners, problem solvers and intellectuals of society. Pip is being raised as a man in society, and is therefore being raised to expect a certain degree of privilege over women in his societal role. His apprenticeship to Joe is described as a 'road to manhood', and it is in learning a craft that he will be able to fulfil the role of 'breadwinner'. That his apprenticeship will place him into a separate male sphere is hinted at early on with Pip's observation in Chapter 2 that 'Joe's forge adjoined our house:' the neighbouring yet removed geographical layout symbolises that the forge is a distinct space from Mrs Joe's female domestic space

[*AO1 for advancing the argument with a judiciously selected quote; AO2 for the close analysis of the language; AO3 for placing the text in historical context*].

- However, having been exposed to the lives of the higher classes through his interactions with Estella and Miss Havisham, this 'manhood' is belittled and invalidated as 'coarse and common'. This comment, coming from a woman, whose role is, societally speaking, supposed to be subservient to man's, can be considered emasculating. That Pip remarks in the above extract that he 'would not have had Miss Havisham and Estella see it on any account' can be seen as symptomatic of this perceived gender imbalance, and motive for his pursuit of gentlemanly status. [*AO1 for advancing the argument with a judiciously selected quote; AO3 for placing the text in historical context*].

Conclusion

Although my third theme had some substantial historical context woven through it, I'm still eager to play it safe and integrate one final nod to AO3 in my conclusion. This time I have done so by invoking another novel by Dickens, and drawing a comparison between a character in said novel and Pip.

"Mr Bounderby in Dickens' earlier novel, *Hard Times* (1854), is an illuminating case study: a wealthy businessman who, in order to make his success appear all the more impressive, conceals his middle class upbringing and affects to have grown up in extreme poverty. Yet whereas Bounderby presents his fictional hardscrabble upbringing as so acutely shameful as to perversely constitute a badge of honour, Pip, who truly experiences a hardscrabble youth, has a more nuanced approach. Pip is portrayed as being ashamed of his social standing at this point in the novel, and is at various points depicted as proud of its escape. However, by the novel's end, he has grown to appreciate his lower-class upbringing not as a shameful origin but one of kindness within poorer means."

An image of Dickens' own birthplace in Portsmouth.

ESSAY PLAN THREE

At this point in the novel, Pip has just moved to London and has asked Herbert to help him become a gentleman.

"I thought he was proud," said I.

"My good Handel, so he was. He married his second wife privately, because he was proud, and in course of time *she* died. When she was dead, I apprehend he first told his daughter what he had done, and then the son became a part of the family, residing in the house you are acquainted with. As the son grew a young man, he turned out riotous, extravagant, undutiful,—altogether bad. At last his father disinherited him; but he softened when he was dying, and left him well off, though not nearly so well off as Miss Havisham.—Take another glass of wine, and excuse my mentioning that society as a body does not expect one to be so strictly conscientious in emptying one's glass, as to turn it bottom upwards with the rim on one's nose."

I had been doing this, in an excess of attention to his recital. I thanked him, and apologised. He said, "Not at all," and resumed.

"Miss Havisham was now an heiress, and you may suppose was looked after as a great match. Her half-brother had now ample means again, but what with debts and what with new madness wasted them most fearfully again. There were stronger differences between him and her than there had been between him and his father, and it is suspected that he cherished a deep and mortal grudge against her as having influenced the father's anger. Now, I come to the cruel part of the story,—merely breaking off, my dear Handel, to remark that a dinner-napkin will not go into a tumbler."

Why I was trying to pack mine into my tumbler, I am wholly unable to say. I only know that I found myself, with a perseverance worthy of a much better cause, making the most strenuous exertions to compress it within those limits. Again I thanked him and apologised, and again he said in the cheerfullest manner, "Not at all, I am sure!" and resumed.

Starting with this moment in the novel, explore how Dickens presents manners in _Great Expectations_.

Write about:

• **how Dickens presents Pip's manners at this moment in the novel.**

- **how Dickens presents manners in the novel as a whole.**

Introduction

This particular essay plan differs slightly from the others. There is a particular argument I'd like to make regarding manners because its central to the novel, yet it is not really dealt with in this particular extract, so the second theme/paragraph in this essay in fact deals exclusively with "elsewhere in the novel." So long as we give sufficient attention to the extract in the other paragraphs, we will still be meeting the exam boards criteria; and I would argue that this essay plan illustrates the flexibility of the thematic method.

"*Great Expectations* concerns an overlap of classes in the form of Pip's social advancement from the position of the adopted son of a blacksmith to gentleman and clerk. Social mobility was not common in the Victorian era, so Pip's (and Dickens', for that matter) position is an unusual one. This enables Dickens to explore upper class expectations of politeness and manner from the perspective of a young man to whom they are new and alien."

Theme/Paragraph One: Pip's lack of understanding of manners is presented as comedic at this moment in the novel and perhaps is a means of endearing those of his social standing to the

educated classes of which Dickens' audience was composite.

- Elsewhere in the novel: Dickens uses a first person retrospective narration from the perspective of an older gentlemanly Pip looking back on the story. Because of this, the narrator allies himself with his upper-class audience via the propriety of tone and genteel language he uses, while the self he is describing performs actions that are neither genteel nor proper. This can be seen clearly in remarks made within the narration such as 'I thanked him, staring at him far beyond the bounds of good manners' (Chapter 10), where the 'bounds of good manners' are familiar to Pip the narrator but not to Pip the character. [*AO1 for advancing the argument with a judiciously selected quote; AO2 for close analysis of the language*].

- In the extract above, when Pip is described as trying to 'pack' his dinner-napkin into his tumbler, this is presented as an ill-mannered and ridiculous endeavour and one of which the narrator is seemingly quite despairing; he confesses he does not know 'why' he was trying to do such a thing and describes its being done 'with a perseverance worthy of a much better cause'. [*AO1 for advancing the argument with a judiciously selected quote*].

- This is one of several faux-pas committed in the extract above all of which are first described by Herbert in dialogue.[1] This device has the effect of centring the reader's attention wholly on what Herbert is saying— in much the way Pip is doing as he absent-mindedly forgets his manners— and presents Pip's bad manners as distractions which are then despairingly confirmed by the narrator. [*AO1 for advancing the argument with a judiciously selected quote; AO2 for discussing how form shapes meaning*].

- These slippages are furthermore not anticipated by the reader, who is primarily focused on Herbert's account of Miss Havisham, meaning his apologetic remarks concerning Pip's manners come as a surprise and lends them a comedic tone further enhanced by the extravagant periphrasis used to describe them.[2] Herbert is being *so* polite in contrast to Pip that his verbose descriptions are themselves ridiculous and comedic: rather than accusing Pip of gulping down his wine, Herbert suggests that one might not be so 'strictly conscientious in emptying one's glass', the use of 'one' here further removing the action from Pip and generalising it. The juxtaposition between Pip's behaviour and Herbert's is presented as stark and humorous. [*AO2 for the close analysis of the language*].

Theme/Paragraph Two: The poor manners of other characters are not presented as quite so endearing, but rather as coarse and disgusting.

- In Chapter 40, when Magwitch returns and is eating breakfast the narrator remarks that 'all his actions were uncouth, noisy, and greedy', and Dickens describes Pip as being 'repelled from him by an insurmountable aversion'. This is a contrast to how Pip reacts to Magwitch's manners when they first meet on the marsh, where they are described as 'most curious' rather than repellent. Since this first encounter, Pip has moved to London and become a

gentleman, distancing him further from the criminal
or vagrant class to which Magwitch belongs. [*AO1 for
advancing the argument with a judiciously selected
quote; AO2 for discussing how structure shapes
meaning*].

- Ironically, despite this social severance, Magwitch's
reappearance in the novel ties the two men together
with greater strength, as it is revealed that Magwitch
is Pip's anonymous benefactor. The escalation in Pip's
appraisal of Magwitch's manners is perhaps evocative
of a greater awareness of politeness combined with an
inability to fully distance himself from the 'low'
nature of his past. Having been called 'coarse and
common' by Estella early on, his motivation
throughout the novel can be considered to be escaping
these roots. Magwitch's confession compromises that
goal. [*AO1 for advancing the argument with a
judiciously selected quote; AO2 for the close analysis
of the language*].

- This is not the first time Pip has been judgmental
towards another character for their manners. In
Chapter 19, he describes Joe as being 'rather
backward in some things' – namely. 'his learning and
his manners'. In both instances, Dickens depicts Pip
as embarrassed about his connections to a lower strata
of society. His repulsion towards Magwitch's manners
may be seen as justified, but Joe is depicted as kind,
loyal and endearing throughout, despite a lack of
education in gentility. By exploring both examples,
Dickens draws out the assumptions made of a person
according to their manners, and challenges his
readership to look beyond a person's gestures and
knowledge of propriety to judge their character. [*AO1*

for advancing the argument with a judiciously selected quote].

Theme/Paragraph Three: Many examples of good/bad manners centre around eating. Although Dickens presents the existence of rules and proper practice surrounding the meals of lower class characters, many of these concerns are more practical than societal.

- Extensive knowledge of manners were a mark of a certain calibre of education in the nineteenth century, and their adherence was expected among the genteel class. Many examples of good manners are ritualistic, and this is certainly true of table manners such as those explored in the extract above, where Pip is learning about the behaviour 'society as a body' expects of him. The phrase 'society as a body' is suggestive of functionalism, a theory which considered society as being like a body, composite of many different parts. If any part of that societal body failed to do its duty the body would become sick or broken. Pip's failure to behave with the table manners suitable for his new class can be seen as evocative of his failure to perform the duty of his part, and is therefore a threat to the well-being of society. [*AO1 for advancing the argument with a judiciously selected quote; AO2 for the close analysis of the language; AO3 for placing the text in historical context*]
- Elsewhere in the novel: 'Society as a body' is not so important to the likes of Magwitch and the Gargery household for whom the corporeal body and its

maintenance is of far greater concern.[3] As Joe puts it in Chapter 2, after he suspect Pip of '[bolting]' his food: 'Manners is manners, but still your elth's your elth'. Similarly Magwitch's greedy and bestial manner of eating is due to a ravenous hunger: he is 'alone on these flats, with a light head and a light stomach, perishing of cold and want'. His priority is not to uphold his manners, but rather to survive. Manners are a luxury. [*AO1 for advancing the argument with a judiciously selected quote; AO2 for the close analysis of the language*].

Conclusion

"Throughout the novel Dickens portrays characters on the margins of class divisions, and their manners do little to demarcate moral calibre. Compeyson, though well-mannered and educated, is still a criminal, and Miss Havisham and Estella are both variously presented as cruel and cold. On the other hand, Joe and Pip are poor of both manner and pocket but are nevertheless portrayed as decent men, strong of moral character and worthy of admiration despite their lack of manners. Ultimately, manners are presented as teachable and are not necessarily signposts of good or moral character, merely of class."

Photographs of Charles Dickens by the photographer
Mathew Brady.

ESSAY PLAN FOUR

READ THE FOLLOWING EXTRACT FROM CHAPTER 28 OF GREAT EXPECTATIONS AND THEN ANSWER THE QUESTION THAT FOLLOWS.

A t this point in the novel, Pip is in a coach on his way to see Joe in the hopes of apologising to him for his behaviour in London.

Cowering forward for warmth and to make me a screen against the wind, the convicts were closer to me than before. The very first words I heard them interchange as I became conscious, were the words of my own thought, "Two One Pound notes."

"How did he get 'em?" said the convict I had never seen.

"How should I know?" returned the other. "He had 'em stowed away somehows. Giv him by friends, I expect."

"I wish," said the other, with a bitter curse upon the cold, "that I had 'em here."

"Two one pound notes, or friends?"

"Two one pound notes. I'd sell all the friends I ever had for one, and think it a blessed good bargain. Well? So he says—?"

"So he says," resumed the convict I had recognised,—"it was all said and done in half a minute, behind a pile of timber in the Dock-yard,—'You're a-going to be discharged?' Yes, I was. Would I find out that boy that had fed him and kep his secret, and give him them two one pound notes? Yes, I would. And I did."

"More fool you," growled the other. "I'd have spent 'em on a Man, in wittles and drink. He must have been a green one. Mean to say he knowed nothing of you?"

"Not a ha'porth. Different gangs and different ships. He was tried again for prison breaking, and got made a Lifer."

"And was that—Honour!—the only time you worked out, in this part of the country?"

"The only time."

"What might have been your opinion of the place?"

"A most beastly place. Mudbank, mist, swamp, and work; work, swamp, mist, and mudbank."

They both execrated the place in very strong language, and gradually growled themselves out, and had nothing left to say.

After overhearing this dialogue, I should assuredly have got down and been left in the solitude and darkness of the highway, but for feeling certain that the man had no suspicion of my identity. Indeed, I was not only so changed in the course of nature, but so differently dressed and so differently circumstanced, that it was not at all likely he could have known me without accidental help. Still, the coincidence of our being together on the coach, was sufficiently strange to fill me with a dread that some other coincidence might at any moment connect me, in his hearing, with my name.

Starting with this moment in the ~~play~~ *novel*, **explore how Dickens presents the importance of coincidence.**

Write about:

- **how Dickens presents coincidence at this moment in the novel.**

- **how Dickens presents the importance of coincidence in the novel as a whole.**

Introduction

In order to ensure you're doing sufficient close reading alongside broader structural analysis for this question, it may be worthwhile compartmentalising your themes into two contrasting analyses of attitudes towards coincidence within the story, and one that considers coincidence as a device used by Dickens.

"Coincidence is a recurrent theme in *Great Expectations*: Pip as the story's protagonist is always in the right place at the right time to overhear, see or experience something that links together the novel's network of other characters. Without his specific but chance placement at particular times, the relationship between Molly, Magwitch and Estella would never have been realised, nor would that between Compeyson and Miss Havisham. Coincidence also facilitates Pip reencountering characters throughout his life at key and formative moments. Whether it is arriving just in time to see Joe and Biddy on their wedding day, or finding the much mistrusted Orlick working as a gatekeeper for Miss Havisham after so strongly suspecting him of assaulting his sister, coincidental meetings also enable Dickens to measure and explore Pip's growing understanding of himself and his relationship to others."

Theme/Paragraph One: Coincidence is depicted as both shocking and dangerous, yet also lucky and fortuitous.

- In this extract, Pip is hearing his own experience being discussed by a group of convicts with whom he happens to be sharing a coach: 'The very first words I heard them interchange as I became conscious, were the words of my own thought, "Two One Pound notes."' It is not only a coincidence that Pip finds himself in this particular coach, but also that he 'became conscious' at exactly the right time to overhear the conversation, and that 'the convicts were closer to [him] than before', thus enabling his eavesdropping. That this particular set of circumstances aligned as such can ultimately be attributed to the weather, as they were only in earshot because they were 'cowering forward for warmth and to make me a screen against the wind'. The weather is a force of nature – the upshot of a

coincidental combination of environmental factors –
and its effect on the passengers in the coach
facilitates a revelation about the mysterious meeting
between Pip, Joe and the man in the pub during his
childhood. [*AO1 for advancing the argument with a
judiciously selected quote; AO2 for the close analysis
of the language*].

- Although this revelation provides closure for Pip on
this particular episode, it also fills him with a dread
'that some other coincidence might at any moment
connect [him], in his hearing, with [his] name'.
Coincidence is therefore also presented as a
dangerous and fearful thing. [*AO2 for the close
analysis of the language*].

- Elsewhere in the novel: It is coincidental that Pip is
found by Magwitch on the marshes in the first
chapter, for example, which was frightening and
dangerous, and further coincidental that it had been
Magwitch and not any of the other escaped convicts.
The other convicts in this extract express incredulity
at the raconteur for not stealing the two pound notes:
'I'd have spent 'em on a Man', and say of Magwitch
that 'He must have been a green one' – that is,
inexperienced and naive. This suggests that
Magwitch's generosity and desire to repay Pip is rare
and particular, and the coincidence of it having been
him that Pip met in the graveyard facilitates Pip later
becoming a gentleman. Coincidence is therefore
presented as both fortuitous but unpredictable and
therefore dangerous. Dickens also suggests that
coincidence breeds coincidence, as Pip fears in the
final line of the extract above. [*AO1 for advancing the*

argument with a judiciously selected quote; AO2 for the close analysis of the language].

Theme/Paragraph Two: Coincidence occurs as a contrast to other fortuitous events in the novel that at first seem coincidental, but are later found out to be orchestrated by another character.

- Elsewhere in the novel: Many other events in the novel are initially presented as coincidental, and are later found out to be part of plans by other characters. For example, it seems coincidental (at least to the likes of Biddy and Joe) that having been filled with dreams of becoming a gentleman, and telling Biddy so – "'Biddy,' said I, after binding her to secrecy, "I want to be a gentleman."' – that in the very next chapter, Mr Jaggers arrives to tell him that he is to become exactly that. It later transpires that this is not, in fact, coincidental at all, and that Magwitch had been saving money and harbouring dreams of repaying Pip for his kindness on the marshes by making him a gentleman. [*AO1 for advancing the argument with a judiciously selected quote; AO2 for discussing how structure shapes meaning*].
- These non-coincidences offer a contrast to the coincidences in the novel. They are facilitated and orchestrated by people like Magwitch and Miss Havisham, not by chance encounters, freak events or natural forces (like the weather in the extract above). It is however often ambiguous at least at first whether strings are being pulled to set events in motion or if they are happening of their own accord.
- In the extract, Pip notes that the convict would only

have been able to have recognised him with the aid of 'accidental help,' which of course does not materialise. This idea of someone or something 'helping' to bring events about may remind the reader that ultimately – whether it be a coincidence of a character's surreptitious machinations that brings an event about – all of these events are all ultimately the result of Dickens' own authorial control, and thus, in a sense, are never coincidences or accidents at all.[1] [AO2 for the close analysis of the language]

Theme/Paragraph Three: Coincidence as a plot device used to create intrigue and tie narrative strands together

- Dickens, within Great Expectations' fictional world, uses coincidence or its appearance in order to maintain suspense and intrigue. The extract above can be seen as one of several episodes in which Dickens foreshadows Magwitch's generosity and thrift. When Magwitch finally reveals himself as Pip's benefactor, though Pip is shocked and repelled, it doesn't seem to contradict the character profile the reader has built for him.

- Like many of his other novels, Dickens released Great Expectations serially, meaning in such a complex and intricately connected plot, it was important to keep certain key characters fresh in the minds of his audience, and furthermore offer them the satisfaction of closure, without giving away any of the later major twists. Here, though the extract above suggests that Pip has finally received closure on this mysterious event from his past, it enables Dickens not only to remind his readers about Magwitch, but also to put him to the back of their attention, as it seems that episode is fully answered and complete. [*AO2 for discussing how structure shapes meaning; AO3 for placing the text in its historical context*].

- Coincidence enables Dickens to put Pip in contact with characters and experiences important for his character development and understanding of his past, without giving away who or what is facilitating his ascension to greater wealth and status.

Conclusion

Although the point about Dickens' writing process is definitely scoring us AO3 marks, I'm eager to ensure that we are picking up all of them; so, once again, I'm starting off my conclusion by invoking the text's literary context.

"Many nineteenth century novels lean heavily on coincidence: the narrative's epistolary existence in Mary Shelley's *Frankenstein,* for instance, depends on a chance meeting between Robert Walton and Victor Frankenstein, and the plots of many of Dickens' other novels (*Oliver Twist; Bleak House*) are riddled with chance events.[2] Sure enough, *Great Expectations* is no exception. Without coincidences, certain links and pieces of knowledge crucial to the novel arc would not be discovered True coincidence also undermines characters' efforts to conceal their actions behind false coincidence and ultimately facilitates discovery and intrigue."

Another poster (this one released to the Chinese market) for the 1946 film adaptation of *Great Expectations*. This one depicts Pip in the graveyard – the location where he coincidentally meets Magwitch for the first time.

ESSAY PLAN FIVE

READ THE FOLLOWING EXTRACT FROM
CHAPTER 35 OF GREAT EXPECTATIONS
AND THEN ANSWER THE QUESTION THAT
FOLLOWS.

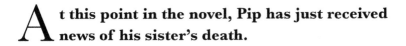

A t this point in the novel, Pip has just received news of his sister's death.

It was the first time that a grave had opened in my road of life, and the gap it made in the smooth ground was wonderful. The figure of my sister in her chair by the kitchen fire, haunted me night and day. That the place could possibly be, without her, was something my mind seemed unable to compass; and whereas she had seldom or never been in my thoughts of late, I had now the strangest ideas that she was coming towards me in the street, or that she would presently knock at the door. In my rooms too, with which she had never been at all associated, there was at once the blankness of death and a perpetual suggestion of the sound of her voice or the turn of her face or figure, as if she were still alive and had been often there.

Whatever my fortunes might have been, I could scarcely have recalled my sister with much tenderness. But I suppose there is a shock of regret which may exist without much tenderness. Under its influence (and perhaps to make up for the want of the softer feeling) I was seized with a violent indignation against the assailant from whom she had suffered so much; and I felt that on sufficient proof I could have revengefully pursued Orlick, or any one else, to the last extremity.

Having written to Joe, to offer him consolation, and to assure him that I would come to the funeral, I passed the intermediate days in the curious state of mind I have glanced at. I went down early in the morning, and alighted at the Blue Boar in good time to walk over to the forge.

It was fine summer weather again, and, as I walked along, the times when I was a little helpless creature, and my sister did not spare me, vividly returned. But they returned with a gentle tone upon them that softened even the edge of Tickler. For now, the very breath of the beans and clover whispered to my heart that the day must come when it would be well for my memory that others walking in the sunshine should be softened as they thought of me.

Starting with this moment in the ~~play~~, *novel*
explore how far Dickens presents Pip's
memory as unreliable. Write about:

• how Dickens presents the reliability of
Pip's memories of his sister at this moment
in the novel.

• how Dickens presents the reliability of
memory in the novel as a whole.

Introduction

This question invites a lot of analysis of Dickens' form and use of narration. Though all plans in this guide follow a thematic approach, this one considers two ways in which the question's suggestion might be true, and then, after summarising, offers a new perspective in its third theme.

"Although primarily classed as a bildungsroman, Dickens writes *Great Expectations* in the style of a fictional memoir, a genre frequently criticised for its idealisation or dramatisation of lived experience and the unreliability of its accuracy. The extract above can be read as an exploration of this theme and Pip's awareness of the changeability of his own memory."

Theme/Paragraph One: *Great Expectations* is written from the perspective of Pip looking back on his life from a position of hindsight. He is both the piece's protagonist and its narrator. This could be seen to call the reliability of his account into question.

- *Great Expectations* is written using a first-person retrospective narration. This means that Pip as a narrator is supposedly writing from a single fixed position in time after the events of the novel are over. Because of this, some of the episodes described were quite far in the past from the time of writing, meaning those memories may not be so fresh and are therefore arguably less reliable. For example, as Pip walks to the forge to his sister's funeral he remembers her cruelty towards him 'vividly'. Indeed, we have previously been told in Chapter 8 that Pip thought of his sister as being 'unjust' to him and confesses that 'I had cherished a profound conviction that her bringing me up by hand gave her no right to bring me up by jerks'. Dickens vague use of syllepsis here highlights the inclination that though Mrs Joe was perhaps kind to take him in, that kindness neither necessitated nor justified her violent treatment of him; the metaphorical 'hand' with which she raised him and for which he is supposed to be grateful, does not excuse the physical hand with which she beats and abuses him.[1] [*AO1 for advancing the argument with a judiciously selected quote; AO2 for the close analysis of the language*].

- Nevertheless, the '[vividness]' of these memories is immediately contradicted by their appearing with 'a gentle tone upon them that softened even the edge of Tickler'. The softening of Tickler – the wax ended cane with which she punished her brother – is a metaphor for the softening of the strength of Pip's resentment towards his sister. The memory of Tickler's strokes seem softer and hurt him less keenly now that time has passed. In this way it can be seen that memory is unreliable as it erodes the strength of emotional experiences. [*AO1 for advancing the argument with a judiciously selected quote; AO2 for the close analysis of the language*].

- Furthermore, Pip seeing himself as a 'a little helpless creature' – though not necessarily untrue – is entirely subjective; he only saw his sister's actions from the perspective of victim. Because the narration is first-person, and we only really encounter Mrs Joe when Pip is a child, we never gain insight into her perspective as we might have with an omniscient narrator. She is not even given a first name. Much of Pip's journey in the novel is about gaining greater understanding of other people and not making assumptions of them according to their class or appearance, but we are never given the opportunity to judge Mrs Joe from any perspective other than Pip's, even though Joe clearly considers her a 'a fine figure of a woman'. Pip's memory can perhaps also be read as unreliable as it is subjective. [*AO1 for advancing the argument with a judiciously selected quote; AO2 for the close analysis of the language*].

Theme/Paragraph Two: Tragedies such as the death of a loved one have a tendency of warping our memories of them. It is perhaps not only time and perspective that renders Pip's memory as unreliable, but also specific events that colour subsequent appreciation.

- Pip's appreciation of his sister can hardly be said to completely reverse following her death; however, it does seem to soften his appreciation of her. Though he could 'scarcely have recalled [her] with much tenderness' the news of her demise brings a 'shock of regret'. Dickens' use of litotes linguistically softens the resentment of which the phrase is suggestive, and though the regret does not come from a place of 'tenderness', he is not happy about the news.[2] The use of the word 'wonderful' to describe the impact the event has on him is archaic and suggests that the impact is momentous and new to him, not that he finds it brilliant that she is dead. [*AO1 for advancing the argument with a judiciously selected quote; AO2 for the close analysis of the language*].

- Elsewhere in the novel: Early in the novel, Dickens also uses the word 'tenderness' in relation to Pip's sister to convey similar feeling prior to her demise: 'I do not recall that I felt any tenderness of conscience in reference to Mrs. Joe'. Here, the narrator is far more divorced from the narrative than in the extract above, since in this context, Pip is still a child. The subject of recollection is the narrator, who is unable to 'recall' feeling any 'tenderness', which is not to say that none was felt. That the narrator here, writing with the knowledge of Mrs. Joe's fate long before it occurs, uses similar wording and syntax is perhaps a sign of a lack of tender recollection on the part of the narrator, not necessarily on the part of Pip as the protagonist. Yet that the narrator is unable to recollect any tenderness is suggestive that he has at least *tried* to do so; he may be unable to recall any tender feelings, but he may also feel as though he should. This may also be in response to the knowledge of Mrs Joe's fate, as in the Victorian era it was seen as highly uncouth to speak ill of the dead. That Dickens, even early on in the novel, softens Pip's indictments of Mrs Joe is perhaps evocative of a respect to her legacy, and a sign that her death had impacted on his recollection.

- Her death further colours his memory of her assault, leading him to 'violent indignation against the assailant from whom she had suffered so much' and renewed anger towards Orlick. Pip's memory of his

sister can be seen as unreliable as it now reimagines
her as a poor victim both of mortality and of previous
violence. Whereas in Chapter 15/16 when she is first
found unconscious, Pip's reaction is one of guilt and
introspection: 'I was a more legitimate object of
suspicion than any one else', 'It was horrible to think
that I had provided the weapon, however
undesignedly', here his renewed fervour towards the
case is directed outwards through anger. [*AO1 for
advancing the argument with a judiciously selected
quote*].

**Theme/Paragraph Three: The above extract may
also be read as a comment on the process of
memory and its changeability. As a fiction rather
than a true memoir, it is self-aware and enables
Dickens to explore the nature of the human
experience.**

- This extract comes from one of the more introspective
  and reflective passages of the book, where the narrator
  is describing the personal internal journey of his past
  self rather than his interactions with other characters.
  These tend to be the more prosaic sections of the
  novel and this is certainly true here. Dickens' narrator
  described his sister's memory as '[haunting]' him even
  though 'she had seldom or never been in [his]
  thoughts of late', and he seems to see her influence
  everywhere, even in places she has never visited: 'In
  my rooms too, with which she had never been at all
  associated, there was [...] a perpetual suggestion of the
  sound of her voice [...] as if she were still alive and had

been often there'. Here memory is depicted as fluid and not discrete to its proper place. Pip's memory can therefore be seen as unreliable as is not a neatly formatted and ordered timeline of experiences, it is pervious to suggestion, association and fancy to the extent that imagination and memory are not so easily separated. [*AO1 for advancing the argument with a judiciously selected quote; AO2 for discussing how structure and form shapes meaning*].

- It is perhaps illuminating to consider the fact that Dickens was a proponent of an early form of hypnotism that appeared in the Victorian era, known as Mesmerism. Given that Mesmerism worked on the basis that the human mind could be altered and manipulated by external stimuli, it is perhaps unsurprising that Dickens conceives of memory to be equally susceptible to suggestion and association. [*AO3 for placing the text in historical context*].

Conclusion

"Ultimately, though Pip's memory is not depicted as especially reliable, the narrator is portrayed as being aware of its unreliability, and the morphing of memory over time, the way it idealises characters and its softening effect on past hardships, resentments and pain are considered as part of the human condition and the process of personal growth. After all, Pip muses that 'the day must come when it would be well for [his] memory that others walking in the sunshine should be softened as they thought of [him]'."

A nineteenth century illustration of *Great Expectations* by F.W. Pailthorpe. The caption below reads: 'Old Orlick means murder,' and it depicts Orlick thrusting a candle before Pip's face.

At this point in the novel, Pip has gone to visit Miss Havisham in the hopes of learning more about Estella's parentage.

She turned her face to me for the first time since she had averted it, and, to my amazement, I may even add to my terror, dropped on her knees at my feet; with her folded hands raised to me in the manner in which, when her poor heart was young and fresh and whole, they must often have been raised to heaven from her mother's side.

To see her with her white hair and her worn face kneeling at my feet gave me a shock through all my frame. I entreated her to rise, and got my arms about her to help her up; but she only pressed that hand of mine which was nearest to her grasp, and hung her head over it and wept. I had never seen her shed a tear before, and, in the hope that the relief might do her good, I bent over her without speaking. She was not kneeling now, but was down upon the ground.

"O!" she cried, despairingly. "What have I done! What have I done!"

"If you mean, Miss Havisham, what have you done to injure me, let me answer. Very little. I should have loved her under any circumstances. Is she married?"

"Yes."

It was a needless question, for a new desolation in the desolate house had told me so.

"What have I done! What have I done!" She wrung her hands, and crushed her white hair, and returned to this cry over and over again. "What have I done!"

I knew not how to answer, or how to comfort her. That she had done a grievous thing in taking an impressionable child to mould into the form that her wild resentment, spurned affection, and wounded pride found vengeance in, I knew full well. But that, in shutting out the light of day, she had shut out infinitely more; that, in seclusion, she had secluded herself from a thousand natural and healing influences; that, her mind, brooding solitary, had grown diseased, as all minds do and must and will that reverse the appointed order of their Maker, I knew equally well. And could I look upon her without compassion, seeing her punishment in the ruin she was, in her profound unfitness for this earth on which she was placed, in the vanity of sorrow which had become a master mania, like the vanity of penitence, the vanity of remorse, the vanity of unworthiness, and other monstrous vanities that have been curses in this world?

Starting with this moment in the novel, explore how Dickens presents extreme emotion in *Great Expectations*.

Write about:

• **how Dickens presents the extremity of Miss Havisham's emotions at this moment in the novel.**

• **how Dickens presents extreme emotions in the novel as a whole.**

Introduction

This question is a great opportunity to flex your AO3 muscles, though make sure you're using your contextual knowledge to platform your analysis, not just as simple recall.

"It is a common misconception that the Victorian period was one that shunned the expression of extreme emotion outright. The propriety of extreme emotion depended on circumstance, company and class; Queen Victoria herself is reported to have wept when she received notice of her ascension to the throne. Although manners and concerns of gentility were rife in the Victorian era, the trope of the British 'stiff upper lip' only fully established itself during the subsequent Edwardian period. There is, furthermore a difference between the experience of extreme emotion and its expression, and this is something Dickens explores throughout the novel through his retrospective first-person narrator."

Theme/Paragraph One: Miss Havisham's extreme emotion is presented as shocking and uncouth.

- Extreme emotions are depicted as a sign of weakness or vulnerability. Pip is described as reacting to Miss Havisham's outburst with 'amazement' and 'terror' and confesses that seeing her in such a state 'gave [him] a shock through all [his] frame'. This can be attributed not only to the previous imperviousness of Miss Havisham's emotional life in particular, but also the expectations of emotional reservation in a woman of both her class and age. He entreats her to rise and calm herself, but her emotions are of such extremity that this proves ineffective. [*AO1 for advancing the argument with a judiciously selected quote; AO3 for placing the text in historical context*].

- Elsewhere in the novel: In contrast, Pip frequently tries to hide his emotions throughout the novel, for instance shortly after this scene in the novel, Pip finds himself feeling 'humiliated, hurt, spurned, offended, angry, sorry,' and begins to cry. However, Estella's delight at 'having been the cause' is described as giving him the 'power to keep them back'. As a young man, Pip has been socially conditioned to be strong and in control of his emotions, ergo, though emotion may be felt extremely, it should not be shown in its extremity.[1] That his ability to hold back his tears is described as 'power' further testifies to the gendered expectation of extreme emotional expression. [*AO1 for advancing the argument with a judiciously selected quote; AO2 for the close analysis of the language*].

- Nevertheless, though Pip is shocked by her outburst, he cannot look at her 'without compassion'. Though her outburst is presented as shameful, the narrator remarks that 'in shutting out the light of day, she had shut out infinitely more; that, in seclusion, she had secluded herself from a thousand natural and healing influences', and therefore treats her with sympathy. Dickens uses quite advanced formal rhetoric here, making extensive use of polyptoton in both the words 'shut'/'shutting' and 'seclusion'/'secluded', which, coupled with a compassionate, though disapproving tone distances the narrator from the actual experience of emotion, from which he has also been distanced by time.[2] The effect of this is that both Pip's real-time reaction, and the narrator's description of it is detached from the experience of emotion. Extreme emotion can be seen in others, but not felt in kind. [*AO1 for advancing the argument with a judiciously selected quote; AO2 for the close analysis of the language*].

Theme/Paragraph Two: Miss Havisham's outburst here is presented as selfish and vain; however, Estella's lack of emotion is not shown in a positive light either.

- Dickens presents Miss Havisham's outburst as highly dramatic and arguably a little performative. He describes in detail her physical gesture: her 'folded hands raised', and how she 'wrung her hands, and crushed her white hair'. These are traditional gestures of distress, and paint a very clear picture of the image of Miss Havisham's emotional outburst. In focussing on the aesthetics of extreme emotion here, Dickens is hinting towards the tradition of codified gesture commonly found in Victorian melodrama, while the elaborate, paragraph-long sentence ensures the form reflects the physical hyperbole. Miss Havisham is repeatedly depicted as melodramatic, the performance of preserving the exact moment of her romantic betrayal is another example. This, coupled with what the narrator describes above as 'the vanity of remorse', invalidates the expression of extreme emotion as performative and selfish. [*AO1 for advancing the argument with a judiciously selected quote; AO2 for the close analysis of the language and for discussing how form shapes meaning; AO3 for using historical context as a means of providing insight*].

- Elsewhere in the novel: Estella in contrast confesses in Chapter 29: 'I have no heart [...] I have no softness there, no—sympathy—sentiment—nonsense'. Furthermore, in response to Pip's declaration of love for her, she states 'I know what you mean, as a form of words; but nothing more.' Pip's extreme feelings for Estella cannot be communicated effectively as they must be filtered through a layer of gesture or speech which she can access intellectually but not emotionally, similar to how Miss Havisham communicates her extreme emotion gesturally but not in a way that enables Pip to engage with the emotions at the gestures' core. [*AO1 for advancing the argument with a judiciously selected quote*].

Theme/Paragraph Three: Extreme emotions are depicted as touching and symptomatic of care.

- Although it has already been observed that Pip in this extract largely comes across as detached, the first part of the rhetorical question he poses – 'And could I look upon her without compassion...' – hints at another way in which extreme emotions are treated in the novel: as a phenomena that might be considered touching. Sure enough, this is how they are depicted elsewhere in the novel. When Pip first leaves the Gargery household he is described as unexpectedly breaking into tears 'with a strong heave and sob'. Rather than depicting this as a shameful moment in the novel, Dickens writes 'we need never be ashamed of our tears, for they are rain upon the blinding dust of earth, overlying our hard hearts'. The righteously prophetic tone of this, is perhaps a means of exploring the class divide between the accepted propriety of extreme emotional expression, and the reference to 'hard hearts' is potentially foreshadowing for Estella's attitudes later in the novel. [*AO1 for advancing the argument with a judiciously selected quote; AO2 for the close analysis of the language*]
- Both Joe and Biddy are also described as emotional here and again at the end of the novel; 'I wept to see her, and she wept to see me; I, because she looked so fresh and pleasant; she, because I looked so worn and white'. Biddy's tears are here emblematic of the concern she feels towards Pip and his sickliness, while Pip's tears are those of appreciation. Regardless of their differing source, these tears are shared and non-performative, the extreme emotion is both expressed

and understood. [*AO1 for advancing the argument with a judiciously selected quote*].

Conclusion

"The way in which extreme emotion is expressed in the novel is depicted as a product of gender, class and upbringing. It can be presented as uncouth and inappropriate if not in response to sufficient aggravation, but elsewhere can be touching and evocative of the tenderness of feeling from one human being to another."

An illustration entitled *Dickens' Dream* by Robert William Buss. Dickens is at his desk and watching a gathering of his fictional characters.

ESSAY PLAN SEVEN

READ THE FOLLOWING EXTRACT FROM
CHAPTER 58 OF GREAT EXPECTATIONS
AND THEN ANSWER THE QUESTION THAT
FOLLOWS.

A t this point in the novel, Pip has recovered
from his illness and has returned home to
thank Joe for his kindness in paying off his debts
and propose to Biddy.

I looked at both of them, from one to the other, and then—

"It's my wedding-day!" cried Biddy, in a burst of happiness, "and I am married to Joe!"

They had taken me into the kitchen, and I had laid my head down on the old deal table. Biddy held one of my hands to her lips, and Joe's restoring touch was on my shoulder. "Which he warn't strong enough, my dear, fur to be surprised," said Joe. And Biddy said, "I ought to have thought of it, dear Joe, but I was too happy." They were both so overjoyed to see me, so proud to see me, so touched by my coming to them, so delighted that I should have come by accident to make their day complete!

My first thought was one of great thankfulness that I had never breathed this last baffled hope to Joe. How often, while he was with me in my illness, had it risen to my lips! How irrevocable would have been his knowledge of it, if he had remained with me but another hour!

"Dear Biddy," said I, "you have the best husband in the whole world, and if you could have seen him by my bed you would have—But no, you couldn't love him better than you do."

"No, I couldn't indeed," said Biddy.

"And, dear Joe, you have the best wife in the whole world, and she will make you as happy as even you deserve to be, you dear, good, noble Joe!"

Joe looked at me with a quivering lip, and fairly put his sleeve before his eyes.

"And Joe and Biddy both, as you have been to church to-day, and are in charity and love with all mankind, receive my humble thanks for all you have done for me, and all I have so ill repaid! And when I say that I am going away within the hour, for I am soon going abroad, and that I shall never rest until I have worked for the money with which you have kept me out of prison, and have sent it to you, don't think, dear Joe and Biddy, that if I could repay it a thousand times over, I suppose I could cancel a farthing of the debt I owe you, or that I would do so if I could!"

They were both melted by these words, and both entreated me to say no more.

"But I must say more. Dear Joe, I hope you will have children to love, and that some little fellow will sit in this chimney-corner of a winter night, who may remind you of another little fellow gone out of it for ever. Don't tell him, Joe, that I was thankless; don't tell him, Biddy, that I was ungenerous and unjust; only tell him that I honoured you both, because you were both so good and true, and that, as your child, I said it would be natural to him to grow up a much better man than I did."

"I ain't a-going," said Joe, from behind his sleeve, "to tell him nothink o' that natur, Pip. Nor Biddy ain't. Nor yet no one ain't."

Starting with this moment in the play, novel explore how Dickens presents familial love.

Write about:

• how Dickens presents familial love at this moment in the novel.

• how Dickens presents familial love in the novel as a whole.

Introduction

The examiner here is asking for analysis of a very specific form of love. Because of this, you need to ensure that your answer is sufficiently focused on familial and not romantic love.

"In Victorian England, the family was seen as an idealised, private sphere which provided a stable retreat from the stresses of industrial work outside the home.

Companionate marriage became more and more the norm throughout the period, with men and women of the same class marrying out of mutual interest or even love rather than for social advancement or familial gain. Meanwhile, the relationship between child and parent varied greatly between classes. In wealthy families, children were primarily raised by nannies and would spend time with their parents only at specific times in the day. In poorer families, children were raised by their parents, but upon reaching sufficient maturity would be expected to go out and earn. Dickens, writing in this context, uses Pip's position as a person who traverses class borders to explore these nuances of class."

Theme/Paragraph One: Joe is presented as the pinnacle of familial love throughout the novel

- Elsewhere in the novel: Dickens presents Pip as being loved deeply by his family, though who that family comprises of varies greatly throughout. There are a number of touching exchanges between Pip and Joe in the early chapters which exemplify the familial love between them. For example, when Joe describes how he accommodated Pip in his plans to marry the subsequent Mrs Joe, the narrator recalls: 'I broke out crying and begging pardon, and hugged Joe round the neck: who dropped the poker to hug me, and to say, "Ever the best of friends; an't us, Pip?"'. [*AO1 for advancing the argument with a judiciously selected quote*].
- Pip never refers to Joe as his father or his brother, nor does Joe describe Pip as his son, but they repeatedly

refer to one another as being 'the best of friends'.
Though this might seem at odds to the concept of
familial love, the specific definition of Joe and Pip's
relationship is somewhat fluid, with Joe taking on the
role of both father and brother but the tenderness
between men in instances such as this are evocative a
strong familial love. The two men do not shy away
from expressing strong emotions, or being vulnerable
around one another; in this instance the infant Pip is
'crying' and in the extract above, Joe has a 'quivering
lip' and seems on the brink of tears. They do not
refrain from physical gestures of affection either; in
the extract above, Joe's hand on Pip's shoulder is
describes as a 'restoring touch', and in the earlier
example, Pip hugs Joe 'round the neck' and Joe drops
the poker in order to return the embrace, signifying
his willingness to abandon his present endeavours to
prioritise Pip. This willingness later reemerges in a
stronger sense when Joe nurses Pip through his
illness, which is referred to in the extract above: 'if you
could have seen him by my bed'. Familial love,
especially between parent and child, can be
considered to be primarily care-orientated, and self-
sacrificing. This can certainly be seen as true in the
case of Joe. Despite disliking London, he remains
there to take care of Pip, and pays off his debts though
he hasn't the wealth of many of the other characters.
[*AO1 for advancing the argument with a judiciously
selected quote; AO2 for the close analysis of the
language*].

- That these two instances are many years and 51
chapters apart shows how Joe and Pip's love for one
another remains constant. Dickens can therefore be

seen to depict familial love as unwavering and steadfast. [*AO2 for discussing how structure shapes meaning*].

Theme/Paragraph Two: Familial love is all-encompassing and is not transactional

- In the extract above, Pip expresses his gratitude to the pair for their generosity in paying off his debts and keeping him out of prison: 'receive my humble thanks for all you have done for me, and all I have so ill repaid'. Pip is extremely self-deprecating in this passage, and promises to pay them back in full, to which they '[entreat]' him to 'say no more.' Their familial love is such that they expect no recompense, despite their generosity. [*AO1 for advancing the argument with a judiciously selected quote; AO2 for the close analysis of the language*].
- Instead, they are simply ecstatic at his visit: 'They were both so overjoyed to see me, so proud to see me, so touched by my coming to them, so delighted that I should have come by accident to make their day complete!' Dickens' use of anaphora here in the word 'so' and the exclamation point at the end of the sentence connotes a sense of overwhelming joy that builds with each new clause. Familial love is presented as accommodating and welcoming in spite of circumstance or hardship. [*AO1 for advancing the argument with a judiciously selected quote; AO2 for the close analysis of the language*].

Theme/Paragraph Three: Familial love is not necessarily dependant on blood relation

- In this extract, Pip sets up a parallel between himself and a hypothetical future son of Joe's and Biddy's to whom he is inferior: 'I hope you will have children to love, and that some little fellow will sit in this chimney-corner of a winter night, who may remind you of another little fellow gone out of it for ever'. Pip further suggests that the child, theirs by birth, would be more likely to share their virtues, and not be 'thankless', 'ungrateful' and 'unjust' as he was: 'as your child [...] it would be natural to him to grow up a much better man than I did'. [*AO1 for advancing the argument with a judiciously selected quote*].

- The insinuation from Pip here is that his relationship to Joe and Biddy is invalidated by his lack of blood relation to them. However, this is swiftly discounted: '"I ain't a-going," said Joe, from behind his sleeve, "to tell him nothink o' that natur, Pip. Nor Biddy ain't."' Here Dickens' use of truncated dialogue in order to qualify the speech with a description of Joe speaking from 'behind his sleeve', adds a sense of weight and measure to the phrase, and contextualises it within an environment of heightened sentiment. The effect of this, following Pip's long meandering sentences, is that Joe's words seem final and conclusive in their simplicity. The inferred meaning here is that Joe will be telling this hypothetical child 'nothink o' that natur', because he does not believe it himself. Dickens therefore presents familial love as being independent of blood relation. [*AO1 for advancing the argument with a judiciously selected quote; AO2 for the close analysis of the language and for discussing how form shapes meaning*].

- Indeed, the one surviving blood relation of Pip's encountered in the novel (before her death in Chapter 34) is Mrs. Joe, Pip's sister. Familial love is not so forthcoming in this relationship. Indeed, a stark comparison is drawn between Pip's feelings for Joe, and those for his sister: 'I do not recall that I felt any tenderness of conscience in reference to Mrs. Joe [...] But I loved Joe'. Here it can be seen that familial love is presented as independent of blood relation, as he '[loves]' his brother-in-law and childhood companion, but feels no 'tenderness' towards his sister. [*AO1 for advancing the argument with a judiciously selected quote; AO2 for the close analysis of the language*].

Conclusion

"Familial love is depicted as one of the strongest bonds within the novel. We encounter marriages that fail and romances that never come to fruition, and bonds of debt that cause anxiety and tension. Familial love is comparatively restorative and unconditional. The most loving familial relationship in the novel is also far less nuclear than the ideals of the Victorian period; that between an orphan and his brother-in-law."

GADSHILL, THE HOME OF CHARLES DICKENS.

Dickens bought Gad's Hill, pictured above, in 1856, and it was his home for the rest of his life. The building is now a school.

ENDNOTES

ESSAY PLAN ONE

1. If you are writing a word phonetically, you are writing it how it sounds as opposed to how it is actually spelt. For instance, the word 'phone' might be spelt 'fone.'

   A regional dialect is phrase to describe how English is spoken in different parts of the country. For instance, people in Yorkshire speak differently to people in Cornwall.

2. In this story, Jesus and his disciples observe people giving to charity at the temple. Although wealthy individuals give large sums of money, Jesus singles out the poor widow who gives a relatively negligible sum, and asserts that her generosity is greatest as she has given a greater proportion of her total wealth.

3. To dissemble is to act or to conceal the truth.

4. The word eponymous basically means that the main character in the book has the same name as the book's title.

ESSAY PLAN TWO

1. The word bildungsroman is in fact German, and, as indicated above, it refers to a coming-of-age story; that is, a story about an individual's formative years.

2. The word hyperbole means something akin to exaggeration. So if something is hyperbolic, it means that it makes use of exaggeration.

3. Anaphora is when you have a word or phrase repeated at the start of a number of clauses in a row. In this case, the phrase that is being repeated is: 'I had believed.'

4. If I were to say, 'the man went to the shop,' that would be the past tense. However, the pluperfect would be if I wrote instead: 'the man had gone to the shop.'

5. If something is bathetic, it means it is anticlimactic.

6. First person narration is when a story is written from a particular character's point of view. This is in contrast to third person narration, where there is an anonymous narrator who is observing the characters go about their business. 'I did this, I went there' is first person, whereas 'she did that, she went there' is third person.

   Great Expectations is a retrospective narrative because Pip is writing as an adult looking back on his life. We call this: looking back in retrospect.

To be omniscient is to be all-knowing. In a sense, the older Pip who is writing this story is all-knowing about the events that will occur in the story.

ESSAY PLAN THREE

1. A faux-pas is when, in a social setting, someone unintentionally or unthinkingly does something that is rude or unseemly.
2. Periphrasis is when someone talks or writers in a really elaborate, round-about and indirect way.
3. The corporeal body basically means the physical body!

ESSAY PLAN FOUR

1. A character's machinations refers to their plans and their attempts to implement them.
2. An epistolaric narrative or novel is one made up of letters written from one character to another. The entirety of *Frankenstein* is ultimately an exchange of letters between an adventurer called Robert Walton and his sister, Margaret Saville.

ESSAY PLAN FIVE

1. Syllepsis is when you have a word in a sentence that seems to have two separate meanings, depending on which part of the sentence you are looking at. The word 'hand' here is metaphorical at first, then literal later in the sentence.
2. Litotes refers to an instance of deliberate understatement. Pip might have said: 'I could not recall her with any tenderness.' However, instead, Dickens has him employ litotes, and Pip says instead that he could 'scarcely have recalled [her] with much tenderness,' and this functions to soften the tone.

ESSAY PLAN SIX

1. Ergo is Latin for 'therefore'!
2. Polyptoton is when you have multiple different words that derive from the same root.

Printed in Great Britain
by Amazon

78448301R00048